THE SERMON ON THE MOUNT

LIVING FOR GOD'S KINGDOM

Other studies in the Not Your Average Bible Study series

Ruth

Psalms

Jonah

Malachi

Ephesians

Colossians

Hebrews

James

1 Peter

2 Peter and Jude

1–3 John

For updates on this series, visit lexhampress.com/nyab

SERMON ON THE MOUNT

LIVING FOR GOD'S KINGDOM

NOT YOUR AVERAGE BIBLE STUDY

MILES CUSTIS

 **BibleStudy** MAGAZINE

 LEXHAM PRESS

The Sermon on the Mount: Living for God's Kingdom
Not Your Average Bible Study

Copyright 2014 Lexham Press
Adapted with permission from content originally published in *Bible Study Magazine*
(Issues 6.4–6.5)

Lexham Press, 1313 Commercial St., Bellingham, WA 98225
LexhamPress.com

ISBN 978-1-57-799571-5

Editor-in-Chief: John D. Barry
Managing Editor: Rebecca Van Noord
Assistant Editor: Abigail Stocker
Cover Design: Christine Gerhart
Typesetting: projectluz.com

CONTENTS

HOW TO USE
THIS RESOURCE

Not Your Average Bible Study is a series of in-depth Bible studies that can be used for individual or group study. Depending on your individual needs or your group pace, you may opt to cover one lesson a week or more.

Each lesson prompts you to dig deep into the Word—as such, we recommend you use your preferred translation with this study. The author used his own translation, but included quotations from the English Standard Version. Whatever Bible version you use, please be sure you leave ample time to get into the Bible itself.

To assist you, we recommend using the Faithlife Study Bible. You can download this digital resource for free for your tablet, phone, or personal computer. Go to FaithlifeBible.com to learn more.

May God bless you in the study of His Word.

INTRODUCTION

The Great Commission tells us to "go therefore and make disciples of all nations" (Matt 28:19), but what does being a disciple entail? The Sermon on the Mount—Jesus' first major teaching in Matthew's Gospel—tells us what it means to be Jesus' disciple and a member of the kingdom of God.

MATTHEW 1:1–6:18

Sitting on the mountainside, Jesus speaks about selflessness, humility and what it means to seek God's righteousness—what we know as the Beatitudes (5:3-12). His disciples should serve as His witnesses to the world and point others toward God (5:13-16). Their standard of righteousness goes beyond what was set forth in the law (5:17-48). In these eight lessons we will examine Jesus' teaching in Matthew 5 to learn what it means to be a disciple of Christ.

THE KINGDOM OF HEAVEN

Pray that the Spirit would give you wisdom as you study the Sermon on the Mount.

Read Matthew 1:1–5:2.

When studying a section of the Bible, it is important to study it in context. As you read the chapters that precede the Sermon on the Mount in Matthew 5–7, pay attention to what Matthew emphasizes. Notice how frequently he points out the fulfillment of Old Testament prophecy. What does this tell you about Matthew's audience? What does it say about Jesus' birth and early ministry?

_____

_____

_____

Think about the key events of Jesus' life as described in Matthew 2–4: the wise men's visit, Jesus' baptism, and His temptation in the wilderness. What do these events reveal about who Jesus is?

_____

_____

_____

Look at Matthew 4:18–25 where Jesus calls His disciples and begins His ministry. What does this passage say about the focus of Jesus' ministry?

_____

_____

_____

John the Baptist and Jesus preached the same message (see 3:1–2; 4:17). The kingdom of heaven, or kingdom of God, is an important concept throughout Matthew. The Sermon on the Mount explains what life in God's kingdom is about—which is later explained through parables in Matthew 13:24–52. Think of how repentance is related to God's kingdom. What must people repent from in order to enter the kingdom?

_____

_____

_____

_____

QUALITIES OF THE KINGDOM

Pray that God would give you humility and a hunger for His righteousness.

Read Matthew 4:18–5:12. Reflect on Matthew 5:1–12.

The Sermon on the Mount opens with nine pronouncements of blessing known as the Beatitudes. They can be understood as requirements for entering God's kingdom or as descriptions of qualities that God approves.

The Greek word for "blessed" (*marakios*, μαχάριος) means "fortunate" or "happy." Look at the characteristics Jesus describes as "blessed" in this passage. What does it mean to be "poor in spirit" (5:3)?

_____

_____

_____

_____

What type of mourning does Jesus refer to in Matthew 5:4 (compare 2 Cor 7:10)?

_____

_____

_____

_____

Whose righteousness should we be seeking (compare Matt 6:33)?

_____

_____

_____

Can you think of opportunities in your life to be a peacemaker (compare Rom 12:14–18)?

_____

_____

_____

After each pronouncement of blessing, Jesus gives a reason ("for ..."). When Jesus describes a quality as "blessed," what is the connection to the reason that follows? What do these reasons have in common?

_____

_____

_____

Throughout the Beatitudes Jesus promotes an attitude of humility. Instead of being powerful or wealthy, the "blessed" people are those who recognize their dependence on God. Which of the qualities listed in Matthew 5:3–12 are evident in your life?

_____

_____

_____

Which qualities do you struggle with?

_____

_____

_____

Spend time praying for forgiveness for the ways you fall short. Consider confessing your failings to a friend and asking them to hold you accountable in these areas.

BEING SALT AND LIGHT

Pray that your life would be an effective witness to those around you.

Read Matthew 4:23–5:16. Reflect on Matthew 5:13–16.

After describing the qualities of those who are part of God's kingdom, Jesus discusses the influence these people can have in the world. He first portrays believers as salt. Ancient Israelites used salt to both flavor and preserve food. How does this metaphor describe believers' relationship with the world?

_____

_____

_____

Why do you think Jesus warns that salt can lose its saltiness? What are some things that can cause you to lose the "saltiness" of your Christian witness?

_____

_____

_____

Jesus also refers to believers as the "light of the world" (5:14). Read Philippians 2:14–16 and Ephesians 5:8–14. What do these passages say about believers being light? What does the contrast between light and darkness imply about how believers should look when compared to the world?

_____

_____

_____

_____

Write a list of the areas in your life where you can reveal God's light. Consider the people in your life who need to see and hear about God's goodness and glory. How can you better display His love?

_____

_____

_____

Jesus specifically mentions "good works" in Matthew 5:16. What should our good works point people toward (see also 1 Pet 2:12)?

_____

_____

_____

If we say we are Christians, our works will say something about God. What do your works reveal about who God is?

_____

_____

_____

RIGHTEOUSNESS TO ENTER THE KINGDOM

Pray that God would give you a greater understanding of His righteousness.

Read Matthew 5:1–48. Reflect on Matthew 5:17–20.

In Matthew 5:17 Jesus shows how God's standard of righteousness extends beyond the righteousness set forth in the Law (see also 5:48). Jesus declares that He came to fulfill the Law and Prophets. Matthew emphasizes Jesus' fulfillment of prophecy throughout his Gospel—but in what way does Christ fulfill the Law?

_____

_____

_____

Read Galatians 5:14, 6:2, and Romans 13:8–10. What does Paul say about fulfilling the Law?

_____

_____

_____

_____

Jesus seems to be advocating a strict legalism in Matthew 5:19. However, the rest of the Sermon on the Mount makes it clear that Jesus cares less about the specific written laws and more about our hearts and how we treat one another (e.g., 7:12).

In Matthew 5:20 Jesus says that only those whose righteousness exceeds that of the scribes and Pharisees will enter the kingdom. The scribes and Pharisees practiced strict obedience to the Law, and they were considered the most righteous groups of Jesus' day. How would someone's righteousness exceed theirs?

_____

_____

_____

Read Romans 9:30–10:4. What different types of righteousness does Paul describe?

_____

_____

_____

What can you do to ensure that you are pursuing God's righteousness and not your own?

_____

_____

_____

ANGER, INSULTS, AND RECONCILIATION

🤚 *Pray that God would keep you from anger and hatred.*

📄 *Read Matthew 5:3–48. Reflect on Matthew 5:21–26.*

After explaining that He is not going to destroy the law (Matt 5:17), Jesus reviews several Old Testament laws and shows how God's requirements actually go beyond the written Law. Those in God's kingdom must have a righteousness that exceeds that of the scribes and Pharisees (see 5:20)— a righteousness that surpasses the Law. Jesus cites Exodus 20:13: "You shall not murder." What does Jesus equate with murder? What does this say about God's standard of holiness?

_____

_____

_____

It seems that we have all insulted someone or become angry at some point in our lives. How do anger and insults relate to murder?

_____

_____

_____

Read Matthew 12:34–37 and 15:16–20. Where does sin originate? Is it easier for you to control your actions or your thoughts and emotions?

_____

_____

_____

In Matthew 5:23-26 Jesus emphasizes the importance of reconciliation, which He portrays as being even more important than worship. How could this teaching be applied today?

_____

_____

_____

If you have offended other believers, what could you do to be reconciled to them?

_____

_____

_____

Read 1 John 3:11-18. What are the consequences of hating another Christian? What does it mean to love "in deed and in truth" (1 John 3:18)?

_____

_____

_____

LUST, SIN, AND MARRIAGE

Pray that the Holy Spirit would keep you from temptation.

Read Matthew 5:13–48. Reflect on Matthew 5:27–32.

Jesus cites the Old Testament law about adultery from Exodus 20:14 but shows that God's requirements go beyond the actual act of adultery to include any lustful thoughts or intentions. By the standard of Matthew 5:28, have you committed adultery?

_____

_____

_____

In Matthew 5:29–30, Jesus talks about the severity of sin. He emphasizes that we should go to great lengths to avoid sin. What are the consequences of not doing so?

_____

_____

_____

Do you take sin as seriously as Jesus seems to? Spend time reflecting on how your sin offends God. Then, bring these sins before God and seek forgiveness for them. Consider confessing your sin to another believer and asking that person to pray for you—especially if you struggle consistently.

_____

_____

_____

_____

Jesus cites a law about divorce from Deuteronomy 24:1–4. Later in Matthew He discusses divorce in greater length. Read Matthew 19:3–9. According to Jesus' teachings in these passages, what is the acceptable reason for divorce?

_____

_____

_____

What reasons did the law allow for divorce?

_____

_____

_____

Jesus stresses the importance of marriage, and Paul compares marriage to Christ's relationship with His Church (Eph 5:22–33). With these teachings in mind, how do you think the faithfulness of Christian marriages can point people to or away from Christ?

_____

_____

_____

OATHS AND RETALIATION

✋ *Pray that God would help you speak honestly and act generously.*

📄 *Read Matthew 5:17–6:6. Reflect on Matthew 5:33–42.*

Jesus quotes a combination of Old Testament laws about swearing oaths (see Lev 19:12; Num 30:2). When the Pharisees made oaths, they would make distinctions between swearing on different items. These distinctions allowed people to get out of the oaths they swore. Read Matthew 23:16–22. What does Jesus say about this practice?

_____

_____

_____

Instead of urging people not to swear falsely, Jesus advocates not swearing oaths at all. Swearing an oath was a way of guaranteeing that what you said was trustworthy. Rather than swearing oaths, Jesus says people should simply be truthful in all their speech. Is your speech honest and trustworthy?

_____

_____

_____

In Matthew 5:38 Jesus quotes the "law of retaliation" found throughout the Old Testament (see Exod 21:23–25; Lev 24:19–21; Deut 19:21). According to Jesus, how should believers act when wronged?

_____

_____

_____

How do you react when someone wrongs you? Do you seek to get even, or do you respond wisely—and even generously—toward the person who has wronged you?

_____

_____

_____

Read Romans 12:17–21. How might a desire for vengeance cause you to be overcome by evil?

_____

_____

_____

PERFECT LOVE

Pray that God would help you love both neighbor and enemy.

Read Matthew 5:17–6:18. Reflect on Matthew 5:43–48.

The final law Jesus cites in this section is from Leviticus 19:18. What words does Jesus remove and add? By doing so, He proposes a radical alternative: loving your enemies. Who would Jesus' audience have considered an enemy?

_____

_____

What is the relationship between "your enemies" and "those who persecute you"?

_____

_____

We probably all have people we would consider enemies in some sense of the word. Do you show love to, and pray for, such people?

_____

_____

_____

We must love our enemies if we are to behave like children of our "Father who is in heaven" (Matt 5:45). Read Romans 5:6–10 and consider how God showed love for His enemies.

_____

_____

_____

Jesus later cites "love your neighbor as yourself" as the second greatest commandment (see Matt 22:36–40), and Paul claims that it fulfills the entire Old Testament law (see Gal 5:14). Why is this commandment so important?

_____

_____

_____

_____

What does it mean to love others "as yourself"? How can you do this better?

_____

_____

_____

_____

Jesus concludes this section of the Sermon on the Mount by promoting an impossible standard: "Be perfect, as your heavenly Father is perfect" (Matt 5:48). Throughout this section (5:17–48) Jesus advocates a righteousness that goes beyond the letter of the law to the spirit of it. How do these requirements show what it means to be perfect?

_____

_____

_____

Read Matthew 19:16–26. What did Jesus say about what is impossible? How might this relate to His statement about being perfect in Matthew 5:48? Understanding that perfection originates from God, how can you ensure you are working toward that goal?

_____

_____

_____

CONCLUSION

In the Sermon on the Mount, Jesus puts forth an impossible standard of righteousness. Not only do we need to guard our actions, we need to guard our thoughts and emotions. Not only should we love our neighbor, we should love our enemy. Jesus calls us to be perfect as God the Father is perfect. Such unattainable aspirations may cause some believers to despair. But this is why Jesus declares the poor in spirit and those who mourn to be "blessed" (see Matt 5:3–4). We cannot achieve God's righteous standard on our own. Only through Christ and His actions can we be part of His kingdom. May you hunger and thirst for God's righteousness, and may you be satisfied by His mercy. Relying on Christ, may you become the disciples He wishes you to be (Phil 4:13).

PART II: THE CALL OF DISCIPLESHIP

MATTHEW 5:1–7:29

It's easy to appear righteous, do good deeds for all to see, and claim allegiance to the Lord (see Matt 6:1–8; 7:21–23). But to uphold God's perfect standard of righteousness (5:20, 48), we must discipline our thoughts, not just our actions (5:21–30). We need to shift our focus from the paths of earthly kingdoms to the ways of God's kingdom (6:19–24).

In the Sermon on the Mount, Jesus explains what it means to follow Him. The road of discipleship is difficult, and it's littered with hypocrites and false prophets. Ultimately, we need faith and reliance on God as we walk this path of discipleship (6:25–33). Following Christ means following His example of selfless love. It means pointing others toward Jesus, the source of our righteousness (5:16). In these eight lessons, we will examine Jesus' teaching in Matthew 6–7. Let's see what it looks like to be an authentic follower of Jesus.

JESUS' SPEECHES IN MATTHEW

Pray that God would give you a heart for others.

Read Matthew 5:1–7:29 aloud.

Reading Jesus' Sermon on the Mount aloud can help you experience it much like the disciples did. It is the first of Jesus' five major teachings in Matthew. The others are in Matthew 10, 13, 18, and 24–25. Look through these chapters to see who the audience is for each speech. What is Jesus' focus in these talks?

_____

_____

_____

Make notes of Jesus' expectations of His disciples (see 10:16–23). Compare Matthew 18:3–6, 18:21–35 and 25:31–46. How does Jesus expect His followers to treat others? How does your life line up with Jesus' expectations?

_____

_____

_____

The Sermon on the Mount marks the beginning of Jesus' public ministry in Matthew's Gospel (following 4:18–25). By the end of the message, "the crowds were astonished at His teaching" (see 7:28–29). In what ways does Jesus establish His authority in this sermon?

_____

_____

_____

The kingdom of heaven, or kingdom of God, is an important concept throughout Matthew. Note what Jesus says about the kingdom in the Sermon on the Mount. What are the characteristics of those in the kingdom? Pray about how you can better exhibit these characteristics in your life.

_____

_____

_____

GIVING WITHOUT HYPOCRISY

Pray that the Holy Spirit would lead you to be generous for God's glory.

Read Matthew 5:13–6:6. Reflect on Matthew 6:1–6.

After promoting a standard of perfect righteousness (see Matt 5:48), Jesus warns against hypocrisy. What is the result of "practicing your righteousness before other people" (6:1)? Compare Matthew 6:1 with 5:14–16. How can you balance practicing righteousness not "in order to be seen" (6:1) but to be a light so that others "see your good works" (5:16)?

_____

_____

_____

Consider the purpose of the good works described in 5:16; how is that description different from the reason for practicing righteousness in 6:1? Good works should glorify your Father in heaven, not yourself.

_____

_____

_____

Jesus discusses specific areas of hypocrisy or self-righteousness in 6:2–6. What does He say about giving to the poor in 6:2–4? When people want others to notice their giving, what reward do they receive?

_____

_____

_____

_____

Reflect upon your actions today and in the past week. Which was more important to you this week: people's praise or God's reward?

_____

_____

_____

Make a list of ways you find yourself pursuing the praise of others more than God. Doing so will help you become more aware of your motives. Then, list ways you can live faithfully for God, and pray about these things.

_____

_____

_____

_____

_____

Jesus doesn't mean that no one should ever know about our charitable giving. Read Acts 4:36–37 and 2 Corinthians 8:1–5. In these passages, we're told about the generosity of Barnabas and the Macedonian churches. They are mentioned to promote similar generosity in others. How can you give generously without drawing attention to your acts of righteousness?

_____

_____

_____

What are some practical things you can do to make sure your actions point people to God?

_____

_____

_____

HOW TO PRAY

Pray the Lord's Prayer (Matt 6:5–15).

Read Matthew 5:17–6:15. Reflect on Matthew 6:7–15.

After warning against hypocritical giving (see 6:2–4), Jesus warns about praying for show. How does He describe praying "like the hypocrites" (see 6:5)?

_____

_____

_____

When Jesus says we should pray privately, with the door shut, He is not speaking against public prayer. He is speaking against prayer that is offered for the sake of being noticed. Read Luke 18:9–14. What do the Pharisee and the tax collector emphasize in their prayers?

_____

_____

_____

_____

Think about how you pray in public and how you pray when you're alone. Do you pray differently? Should you? When you pray publicly, how can you make sure that you're exalting God and not yourself?

_____

_____

_____

_____

In 6:7–8 Jesus instructs His disciples not to pray with empty, repeated words like the Gentiles do. What reason does He give?

_____

_____

_____

_____

_____

If God knows what you need before you ask Him, then why pray at all?

_____

_____

_____

_____

Read Romans 12:12, Ephesians 6:16–19, Philippians 4:6, Colossians 4:2, and 1 Thessalonians 5:17. What does Paul say about prayer in these passages?

_____

_____

_____

_____

Read Luke 18:1–8. What does this parable say about being persistent in your prayers? Pray that God will show you how to become more diligent in your prayer life.

_____

_____

_____

_____

Matthew 6:9–13 is known as the Lord's Prayer. The plural voice throughout ("our," "us," we") indicates it is meant to be a corporate prayer. What does Jesus emphasize about God in this prayer (see 6:9–10)? What are the implications of calling God "our Father" (compare Gal 4:4–7)?

_____

_____

_____

_____

What requests does Jesus make in this prayer (see Matt 6:11–13)? What petitions do you bring to God in prayer?

_____

_____

_____

_____

TWO KINDS OF TREASURE

Pray that God would help you focus on treasures in heaven.

Read Matthew 5:17–6:24. Reflect on Matthew 6:16–24.

Jesus finishes His discussion of hypocrisy and goes on to describe genuine fasting. Similar to His teaching about giving to the poor and praying (see 6:2–6), Jesus warns against fasting in a way that draws attention to your own righteousness. In Jesus' era, fasting typically occurred along with prayer or worship and was often related to the confession of sins or seeking God (compare Deut 9:18; 2 Sam 12:16; 2 Chr 20:3–4; Luke 2:37; Acts 13:2–3).

In 6:19–24 Jesus contrasts earthly treasures with heavenly treasures. How does this passage relate to Jesus' discussion of hypocrisy in 6:1–6 and 6:16–18?

_____

_____

_____

_____

_____

The phrase "treasures on earth" includes wealth and possessions, but it can also include the approval and praise of others (see 6:2). What kind of earthly treasures do you regularly seek? Pray about ways you can keep yourself from seeking earthly treasures (see Heb 13:5–6).

_____

_____

_____

_____

_____

What does it mean to "lay up treasures in heaven" (Matt 6:20)?

_____

_____

_____

_____

Compare Matthew 19:16–22 and 25:31–46. Jesus uses the heart and the eye
to illustrate a person's priorities (6:21–23). Psalm 25:15, 26:3, 40:8, and 119:111
explain these analogies. What do you set your eyes and heart on?

_____

_____

_____

_____

DON'T WORRY

Pray that God would help you have faith in both small and big matters.

Read Matthew 6:1–34. Reflect on Matthew 6:25–34.

In 6:25 Jesus begins a discussion on worry by pointing back ("therefore...") to what He just said. How does Jesus' teaching on worry relate to the accumulation of earthly treasures?

_____

_____

_____

_____

What worries does Jesus mention in 6:25? What aspects of life cause you to worry?

_____

_____

_____

_____

Jesus uses two illustrations from nature to explain why we shouldn't worry: Birds don't store up their next meal, but God provides for them; lilies don't exert any effort to grow, but God makes them beautiful. Jesus does not say we should neglect planning ahead or being diligent in our work (compare Prov 10:4–5). Instead, He says we should not be anxious or worry about these matters.

In Matthew 6:27 Jesus says worry cannot accomplish anything. What is the relationship between worry and faith (see 6:30; 8:26; 14:31)?

_____

_____

_____

_____

Is it easier for you to have faith in God for big concerns—things like salvation—than for everyday concerns? Explain your answer.

_____

_____

_____

_____

What does Jesus say we should do instead of worrying (6:32)?

_____

_____

_____

_____

How do we go about seeking the kingdom (compare 5:3-12, 19-20)? Pray about how you can seek what is important to God's kingdom and not worry about your own safety or security.

_____

_____

_____

_____

JUDGING, ASKING, AND THE GOLDEN RULE

🙏 *Pray that the Spirit would show you your faults.*

📄 *Read Matthew 6:1–7:12. Reflect on Matthew 7:1-12.*

In 7:1–6 Jesus warns against judging. Does Jesus' command to not judge mean we should never confront someone about their sin?

_____

_____

_____

Compare Matthew 18:15-20, 1 Corinthians 5:11–13, Galatians 6:1, and 2 Thessalonians 3:14-15. What do we learn in these passages about confronting sin in a fellow believer?

_____

_____

_____

Jesus elaborates on His command to not judge with the illustration of the speck and the log (see Matt 7:3-5). Do you have a tendency to notice others' faults while ignoring your own? Think of ways you can focus more of your attention on your own faults.

_____

_____

_____

_____

Jesus speaks of God's generosity in 7:7–11. He encourages His disciples to ask, seek, and knock, promising that God will "give good things to those who ask Him" (7:11). Jesus is not saying that God will give you whatever you ask for. How might God's understanding of good things differ from yours? Read Hebrews 12:5–11.

_____

_____

_____

Matthew 7:12 is known as the "Golden Rule." According to Jesus, this rule fulfills the Law and the Prophets (see also 22:37–40). Similar statements appear in other traditions but are often presented in the negative: "do not do to others what you would not want done to yourself." How does framing it positively ("do") instead of negatively ("do not do") change the focus? Which is easier to follow?

_____

_____

_____

_____

THE NARROW PATH

✋ *Pray that others will recognize "good fruit" in your life.*

📄 *Read Matthew 6:19–7:23. Reflect on Matthew 7:13–23.*

As Jesus nears the conclusion of His sermon, He describes two gates or paths (7:13–14). The narrow gate leads to life, but this path is difficult because it requires us to uphold God's perfect standard of righteousness (see 5:20–48). How can anyone walk this path? Elsewhere, Jesus describes Himself as the gate (John 10:9). Only through Jesus can we walk the narrow and difficult way.

_____

_____

_____

In Matthew 7:15–20, Jesus warns about false prophets. How can we recognize them? What are some "fruits" to look for?

_____

_____

_____

_____

Read Galatians 5:22–24. Do you exhibit the fruit of the Spirit in your life? Would people recognize you as a Christian by your fruit?

_____

_____

_____

_____

Jesus explains that many people expect access to the kingdom of heaven but will be turned away (see Matt 7:21–23). It's not enough to claim things in God's name. Instead, we must do the will of the Father—but what does that mean?

_____

_____

_____

How can you be sure that you are doing God's will and are not among those falsely calling on His name (compare Jesus' discussion of hypocrisy in 6:1–18)?

_____

_____

_____

A SURE FOUNDATION

🖐 *Pray that God would make you a doer and not just a hearer of His Word.*

📄 *Read Matthew 7:1-29. Reflect on Matthew 7:24-29.*

Jesus concludes the Sermon on the Mount with an illustration showing the proper response to His teaching. He contrasts a wise man who built his house on rock with a foolish man who built his house on sand. Have you built your life on rock or sand?

_____

_____

_____

A few verses earlier, Jesus spoke of the difficulty of following Him (see 7:13-14). Here, He speaks of the importance of following His teaching—hearing alone is not enough. Read James 1:22-25. How does James describe people who are hearers of the Word and not doers?

_____

_____

_____

_____

What is involved in being a doer of the Word?

_____

_____

_____

_____

Read through the Sermon on the Mount and highlight Jesus' commands. How can you remind yourself to practice these things in your life?

_____

_____

_____

In Jesus' illustration in Matthew 7:24-27, both houses endured a heavy rainstorm with winds and flooding. What might these storms represent in your life?

_____

_____

_____

Read the parable of the Sower in 13:3–9 and 13:18–23. What would you identify as "storms" in this parable?

_____

_____

_____

How does being a doer of the Word help you endure persecution or avoid being trapped by the cares of the world?

_____

_____

_____

CONCLUSION

When Jesus concluded the Sermon on the Mount, the crowd was astonished. They had not heard anyone teach with such authority (Matt 7:28-29). Yet Jesus' authority was demonstrated not only in His teaching, but in His actions. Through His miracles, He demonstrated His authority to forgive sins (9:1-7). His resurrection proved that He could conquer sin and death. He provided salvation for the world and served as the perfect example of obedience. Jesus didn't just preach the Sermon on the Mount—He demonstrated how to live it throughout His life. When Jesus calls us to go beyond hearing His words to acting on them, He does so as one who perfectly followed what He taught. This is why the author of Hebrews encourages us to look to Jesus as we "run with endurance the race that is set before us" (Heb 12:1-2). The road is not easy, but we can do all things through Christ (Phil 4:13). May you follow Christ's example and be a doer of His words.

Make Your Bible Study Even Better

Get 30% off Bible Study Magazine.

Subscribe today!

BibleStudyMagazine.com/Subscribe

1-800-875-6467 or +1-360-527-1700 (Int'l)